CW00760741

THE
BLIND MAN
WITH THE
LAMP

TASOS LEIVADITIS

THE
BLIND MAN
WITH
THE LAMP

Translated
& introduced
by
N. N. TRAKAKIS

DENISE HARVEY (PUBLISHER) · LIMNI, EVIA, GREECE

First published in 2014 by Denise Harvey (Publisher)
340 05, Limni, Evia, Greece

The Blind Man with the Lamp was first published in Greek
by Kedros Publishing, Athens, in 1983
with the title *Ο Τυφλός με τον Λύχνο*

Cover design by Maria Tsirodimitri
Cover photograph of Tasos Leivaditis by courtesy of Stylianos-Petros Halas

The Blind Man with the Lamp
is the twentieth publication in
THE ROMIOSYNI SERIES

The books published in the Romiosyni Series are concerned with the
forms and expressions of Greek life and culture that emerged during the
post-Byzantine period while still remaining deeply rooted in what is
often referred to as the 'Greek East'. This life and culture is often
identified by the enigmatic word *Romiosyni*, which derives from the
connection of the Greeks with 'new Rome' — Constantinople — and
the Eastern Roman Empire. People who dwelt within this Empire called
themselves *Romioi* — Romans — hence *Romiosyni*, which in a non-
nationalistic sense could be rendered as Hellenism.
Romiosyni is a word that has both historical and emotional
connotations and expresses for the modern Greek a particular aspect
of his national identity. Historically, this identity was not limited to a
political, racial or territorial boundary, and this sense of nationality
depended more on the sharing of a certain milieu, almost a state of
mind, than on anything else.

For more information about these books, please visit

www.deniseharveypublisher.gr

ISBN 978-960-7120-32-8

CONTENTS

TRANSLATOR'S NOTE

I gratefully acknowledge the permission granted by Kedros Publishing and by the sole owner of the literary rights to Tasos Leivaditis's works, Mr Stylianos-Petros Halas, to publish this collection in English translation. I would also like to thank Helen Nickas and Denise Harvey, both of whom read and commented upon the entire translation, in the process rescuing me from many errors.

I dedicate this translation to M. G. Micheal, who introduced me to the work of Leivaditis.

TASOS LEIVADITIS:
HIS TIMES AND HIS WORK

TASOS LEIVADITIS is one of the unacknowledged greats of Modern Greek literature — unacknowledged not only in the English-speaking world, where his work is barely known largely because nearly all of it remains untranslated, but also unacknowledged within modern Greek literary circles, where he is often overshadowed by twentieth-century giants such as Cavafy, Seferis, Elytis, Ritsos and Kazantzakis, who have become established names in the literary world at large. Even today, Leivaditis is, I suspect, quickly assimilated into the poetry of the post-war generation, thus effectively silencing the profound ways in which his writing grapples with but also transcends the struggles and concerns of a particular epoch. At his best, Leivaditis speaks to the heart and condition of the whole of humanity, in all its sorrowful joys, with a special gift for depicting and arousing its core: the life of love, or *eros*. A contemporary of his, and an important poet in his own right, Titos Patrikios, has put this wonderfully well:

> Tasos Leivaditis's life was poetry. Not that he made a living out of poetry — very few have managed that and even then only late in their careers. Nor was his a life of poetry only, as with other poets. For his life was one of love [*erota*], or more precisely loves, which constantly shook him up, either giving him a new lease of life or breaking his heart. He lived with the dream of revolution and with the nightmare of its defeat. He lived with the drama of the oppressed, whether they be near to him or distant, and with the anguished immersion into his own self. He lived the joys of intimate relations with family and friends, and at the same time the tormenting desire of

escape from every form of attachment. He lived conversing with ordinary folk he'd meet in his neighbourhood or at 'the crossroads of the world', and he would also talk with the dead, always having something to tell them, no matter how belated. He lived savouring sensations and pleasures, while also punishing himself for actual or imaginary sins. But all this, and other things besides which we'll never know, came to nourish his poetry. A close reading of his works will suffice to make this process crystal clear.[1]

*   *   *

Tasos Leivaditis — or, to give his full name, Panteleimon Anastasios Leivaditis — was born in Athens on 20 April, the eve of Easter Sunday, in 1922, a momentous year in modern Greek history. Leivaditis's mother (Vasilike Kontopoulos) was an Athenian, while his father (Lysandros) hailed from Arcadia in the Peloponnese and became a prosperous textile merchant in Athens. Tasos shared the family home, located in the suburb of Metaxourgeio, with four older siblings: one sister (Chrysaphenia), two brothers (the eldest Alexandros, and Dimitris), and a half-brother (Konstantinos) from his mother's previous marriage. Two of his brothers were to become artists: Dimitris turned to music, while Alexandros became a successful actor in theatre and film. (The artistic legacy was to be passed on to Tasos's nephew, Thanos Leivaditis (1934–2005), an acclaimed actor and screenwriter.)

Tasos's early years seem to have been exceptionally happy: 'O childhood! Eternity untranslatable' he was to exclaim in a posthumously published poem.[2] Such sentiments are

[1] Titos Patrikios, 'Prologue' to Tasos Leivaditis, *Greek Poets* [in Greek] (Athens: Kastaniotis, 2005), p. 11 (translation mine, as are all other texts translated from the Greek that follow).

[2] 'Daybreak', from the collection entitled *Autumn Manuscripts*, published posthumously in 1990. See Leivaditis, *Poetry, vol. 3: 1979–1990* [in Greek] (Athens: Kedros, 2003), p. 491.

corroborated in the following account given by a close high school friend, Nikos Drettas:

> Tasos made a mark on my life. He imbued it with value. His childhood years were passed in a carefree manner. Since he was his mother's youngest child, she would indulge all his whims. In this way, my friend grew up much loved, but also with unlimited freedom. No-one sought to oppress him. Just imagine: from fourteen years of age he would return home at night whatever time he wished! He was not a diligent student. He was a dreamer — as a child, as an adolescent, and as an adult. And he lived life with passion. He was very much taken in by women — eros. He was deeply erotic — in both his poetry and his life. He was handsome too.[1]

By all reports his good looks were enhanced by his sense of style; he would always make the effort to dress well, this earning him the nickname 'Lord Byron'. Music also played an important part in his early years, and he took lessons at home with his brothers and became adept at the piano and violin.

But by the time Leivaditis had begun high school, in 1934, dark clouds were enveloping Greece stemming from events that had taken place late in 1922. In August-September of that year the Turkish army led by Mustafa Kemal (Atatürk) had dramatically defeated the Greek forces in Asia Minor, pushing the Greeks back to Smyrna and indeed out of Smyrna, killing Greeks and Armenians and burning and destroying the Christian parts of the city. This was the 'Asia Minor Catastrophe' that put a final end to the 'Great Idea', the long-held hope of an expanded Greek empire with Constantinople as its capital. In the 'exchange of populations' formalized in the Treaty of Lausanne in July 1923, over one

---

[1] Quoted in Lefteris Papadopoulos, 'Texts with Soul', in Tasos Leivaditis, *Great Figures of Literature: Their Life, Times and Work* [in Greek] (Athens: Kastaniontis, 2008), pp. 9–10.

million Greeks were forced to leave Smyrna and go to Greece in exchange for 380,000 Turkish Muslims established in Greek territory, who were compelled to leave for Turkey. As a result of this policy, the population of Greece, and especially of Athens, rose markedly and quickly. Athens was 'encircled by refugee shanty towns which survived for many decades afterwards'[1] — and it was this Athens that Leivaditis was raised in and came to know at close hand.

The crisis in Asia Minor was to bring about a period of great political instability in the 1920s, which no doubt gave the young Leivaditis a sense and foretaste of the turmoil of Greek politics. Conflicts over Greece's response to the outbreak of World War I in 1914 gave rise to what was to become a 'national schism' between the (progressive) Venizelists and the (conservative) Royalists. After the Asia Minor debacle and the recriminations that followed, the schism was reignited and, in late 1922, King Constantine abdicated as a military junta seized power. A plebiscite in 1924 officially made Greece a republic, while the following year another military dictatorship, that of General Pangalos, came to power. It was only when Pangalos was overthrown and, in 1928, Eleftherios Venizelos won the elections by a massive majority that the country entered a period of relative peace and stability.

The turmoil of the 20s, however, was to return in the mid-30s, by which time Venizelos had left office and the monarchy was restored in controversial circumstances. In the midst of a worldwide depression, which had devastating repercussions on Greece (forcing her to default on interest payments in 1933), Greek politics was again in a downward spiral. The 1936 elections produced a stalemate between the two main parliamentary blocs, the Venizelists and the Royalists, and this

[1] Richard Clogg, *A Short History of Modern Greece* (Cambridge: Cambridge University Press, 1979), p. 121.

paved the way for yet another military dictatorship, this time led by General John Metaxas. It would be ten years before parliament was reconvened, and during this time communists were ruthlessly persecuted. This itself suggests that the Left was now playing a significant part in Greek politics and society, even holding the balance of power after the 1936 elections, and the rise and mistreatment of communists must have made a lasting impression on Leivaditis as a high school student.

It was not only the state of politics, but also the state of literature in the decades prior to World War II that had a formative role in shaping Leivaditis's writing. Literature in the 1920s was, like politics, in an impoverished condition. As one commentator put it, 'The Asia Minor disaster in 1922 found modern Greek literature at the most thankless hour of a painful adolescence.'[1] The poet Kostis Palamas (1859–1943), a towering figure in modern Greek letters, was still writing after 1920, but his most creative work was behind him. Indeed, the younger generation wished to throw off the weighty and stifling influence of Palamas and strike out in their own direction, often absorbing in their more cosmopolitan outlook currents from beyond the national borders. From Alexandria came the poems of Cavafy, discovered and celebrated by the young in 1920s Athens, while from Paris surrealist poetry was introduced to Greece, first by Andreas Embeirikos (1901–75), followed prominently in painting as well as poetry by Nikos Engonopoulos (1907–85) and to a lesser extent by Odysseus Elytis (1911–96). Another Western import that was to have a great impact on Greek literature (as it did in Greek politics) was Marxism, evident in the conversion of many Greek intellectuals and poets to Marxism around this time; for example, Kostas Varnalis embraced Marxism after going to Paris in 1919 on a state scholarship,

---

[1] C. Th. Dimaras, *A History of Modern Greek Literature*, trans. Mary P. Gianos (London: University of London Press, 1972), p. 487.

and Nikos Kazantzakis turned from nationalism to communism in the early 1920s. These currents, above all surrealism and communism, left an indelible mark on Leivaditis.

Leivaditis's work was equally, if not more directly, inspired by the formidable 'generation of the 30s', an influential group of poets (spearheaded by George Seferis, Elytis and Yannis Ritsos) and novelists (including Stratis Myrivilis and George Theotokas) who reinvigorated Greek literature after the cultural degeneration brought about by the Asia Minor disaster. In the manifesto of this generation, Theotokas's 1929 essay *Free Spirit*, Theotokas wrote: 'Our elders had sunk in the port of Smyrna not only their strength but also their ideals and their self-confidence.'[1] This mood of disillusionment and pessimism, conjoined with attitudes of irony, scepticism and anti-heroism, came to displace the exalted odes and aspirations of previous generations. Nowhere is this more apparent than in Kostas Karyotakis (1896–1928), whose bitter and sarcastic poems conveyed the gap between the old ideals and the new reality. After Karyotakis's suicide in July 1928, a spirit of decadence and decay — 'Karyotakism' — swept through the periodicals and cafés, fed by an array of minor poets who, in the words of the scholar Constantine Trypanis, were 'dubious heirs' of Karyotakis, characterized as they were by 'their denial of moral values and their conviction that misery and disillusion were a kind of divine gift.'[2]

Out of this nihilist climate arose the 1930s generation, forging new paths in Greek literature by combining the Greek literary tradition with modernist trends. George Seferis (1900–71) marked the transition with his aptly-titled collection, *Strophe* (*Turning-Point*, 1931), a group of rhymed lyrics strongly influenced by the French symbolists; and in

[1] George Theotokas, 'Free Spirit', trans. Soterios G. Stavrou, *Modern Greek Studies Yearbook* 2 (1986): 191.
[2] C. A. Trypanis, *Greek Poetry from Homer to Seferis* (London: Faber and Faber, 1981), pp. 686–7.

Mythistorima (*Myth-History*, 1935), indebted to the techniques employed by Eliot and Pound, Seferis left behind metre and rhyme, and developed his own style through free verse. But it was the life and work of Seferis's contemporary, Yannis Ritsos (1909–90), that was to provide a more instrumental model for Leivaditis. Ritsos's life, like that of Leivaditis's (as we will soon see), was difficult and turbulent — but it was precisely this that inspired Ritsos's profound concern for freedom and justice, which he expressed in a voluminous output of more than a hundred works. These writings, including poetry, plays, novels and essays, were consistently informed by a commitment to the political Left. Ritsos joined the Greek Communist Party (KKE) in 1934 and remained a lifelong member, fighting with communist guerrillas during the Nazi occupation of Greece and the subsequent civil war. It was this alliance with the communists that led to his lengthy incarceration in political prisoner camps — a fate he shared with Leivaditis.

In 1940 Leivaditis enrolled in the Law School of the University of Athens, and later that year, on 28 October, Greece entered World War II after Metaxas's famous response of '*Ohi*' ('No') to the request of the Axis powers for access through Greece. The Greek resistance, however, could not hold back Hitler's troops, and by June 1941 Germany had control of the country. The occupation was a time of horrific hardship for the Greeks, who were exposed to an appalling famine in Athens during the 1941–42 winter resulting in around 100,000 deaths. In 1943 Leivaditis lost his father, who had previously been reduced to economic bankruptcy. That same year Leivaditis abandoned his studies and joined the resistance — specifically, the youth wing of the communist resistance movement, known as the National Liberation Front or EAM (*Ethnikon Apeleftherotikon Metopon*). Non-communist resistance groups were also formed (the most important being the National Republican Greek League, or

EDES: *Ellinikos Dimokratikos Ethnikos Stratos*), but communist and non-communist groups rarely co-operated and even fought against one another, thus giving rise to a civil war within the broader war. Leivaditis himself, soon after joining the communist resistance, was arrested and imprisoned by non-communist authorities for 45 days.

Once the Germans withdrew in October 1944, the Greek government led by George Papandreou returned from exile. But the gulf between right and left in Greece was widening, and leftists were often subjected to persecution of various forms. Thus Greece entered into war again, not a Cold War as elsewhere, but an actual Civil War beginning in the winter of 1946–47 between communist forces and the regular army, with Leivaditis again joining the communists. This war, as Richard Clogg has stated, 'added a whole new dimension of hatred and division to the Greek tragedy.'[1]

In 1946 Leivaditis married his childhood friend, Maria Stoupas, who was to stand by him through many a difficult period. (They were to have one daughter: Vasiliki.) In one of his early works, *This Star Is For All of Us* (1952), Leivaditis not only dedicates the work to Maria but makes her the focus of the poem, movingly expressing his undying love for her. Also in 1946, Leivaditis published his first literary work: a poem 'The Song of Hatzidimitri' in the periodical *Elefthera Grammata*.

As the Civil War was drawing to a close, the successes of the national army meant that those fighting on the opposing side were to face harsh penalties for their political commitment. Leftist artists such as Yannis Ritsos, Aris Alexandrou and Manos Katrakis were arrested and exiled to camps. In June 1948 the same fate befell Leivaditis, who was detained in camps in Moudros (a town on the island of Lemnos), Makronisos (an island in the Aegean Sea), and then Aghios-Eustratios (a small island in the northern Aegean Sea). It was

[1] Clogg, *A Short History of Modern Greece*, p. 164.

while he was exiled in Makronisos that he learned of the death of his mother, whom he greatly adored, as is apparent in many of his poems. He was finally transferred to a prison in Athens, from which he was released in 1951, having by that time spent over three years in detention.

During his years in prison Leivaditis did not cease writing, but only after his release could he again publish his work. His first poetry collections were published in 1952: *Battle at the Edge of the Night* and *This Star Is For All of Us*. Both were instant successes. The former consists of a single, extended account of the horrors experienced during the night by a soldier plunged in the depths of a vicious war, and opens with these haunting lines:

> *Brother, are you here?*
> *I can't see you in the dark*
> *and this corporal*
> *he is late*
> *what time is it?*
> *I'm cold.*
>
> *I'm cold too*
> *light up a match*
> *what time is it?*
> *how are we to believe again in the world?*
> *what time is it?*
>
> *The gate is bolted*
> *the road deserted*
> *like discarded bones*
> *the outposts in the dark*
> *and this corporal*
> *my God*
> *he is late*
> *why does the wind blow?*

What time is it in the dark?
what time is it in the rain?
what time is it today on all the earth?
What time is it?[1]

The following year, 1953, there followed another lengthy poem, *The Gust at the Crossroads of the World*, for which he was awarded first prize in poetry at the World Youth Festival in Warsaw.

By this time Greece had entered another deeply right-wing phase in politics: General Papagos's party won the 1952 elections and instituted eleven years of right-wing rule in Greece. Although this was a period of social and economic reconstruction in a war-torn land, repressive measures and attitudes against communists continued. In December 1953, for example, Leivaditis's *The Gust at the Crossroads of the World* was confiscated and banned by the censors who deemed it a 'subversive proclamation', and later Leivaditis was arrested and brought before the courts. The proceedings, which took place in February 1955, were followed by a great crowd, including many literary figures. In the dock Leivaditis presented a spirited defence of his work, touching not only the audience but also the judges, who ended up acquitting him.[2]

The publication in 1956 of Leivaditis's *The Man with the Drum* brought to an end the first period of his poetic work, during which time he developed a 'poetry of the battlefield' (as it has been dubbed), much influenced by Ritsos. The epic and lyric quality of Leivaditis's early poetry serves to evoke, in the spirit of socialist realism, the horrors and devastation of

---

[1] Leivaditis, *Poetry, vol. 1: 1950–1966* [In Greek] (Athens: Kedros, 2003) pp. 11–12.

[2] Leivaditis often drew upon this experience in his poetry, as well as in a wonderful short story entitled 'Capital Punishment', included in his 1966 collection of short stories *The Pendulum* (in Greek).

xviii

war while also retaining an optimism regarding the future vindication of the struggle. Leivaditis thus became an important member of the first generation of postwar poets, including also Aris Alexandrou (1922–78) and Manolis Anagnostakis (1925–2005), whose politicized poetry reflects their grim and traumatic wartime experiences. Unfortunately this political commitment often manifests itself as rhetoric or propaganda, and Leivaditis's work during this period is not free from such ideological blinkers, to that extent rendering it compromised and unconvincing.

In 1957 Leivaditis entered the second phase of his oeuvre, publishing his award-winning *Symphony #1* on the struggles of postwar life in the midst of economic and social reconstruction. Further publications — including *The Horse-Eyed Women* (1958), *Cantata* (1960), exhibiting the close correspondence Leivaditis's work has often had with musical and theatrical works, and the lengthier *Poems: 1958–1964* — signalled more definitively the new turn his writing was taking. In the aftermath of the defeat of the Left in the Civil War, Leivaditis's poetic vision took on a bleaker and disillusioned tone, contributing to the rise of the new genre of 'poetry of defeat'. The futility of previous battles for a better world is now highlighted, while existential concerns and even religious imagery become more prominent, as when depicting 'a world torn asunder / with a derelict God who would go around from door to door / begging for his existence.'[1] With the war over, another and more desperate war begins, an

---

[1] Leivaditis, 'Genesis (Version 3)', *Poems: 1958–1964*, in *Poetry, vol. 1: 1950–1966*, p. 408. It seems that many other poets at this time were similarly turning to the centuries-old language and tradition of Orthodoxy. Elytis published *To Axion Esti* (1959, *Worthy It Is*), Seferis wrote his final collection, *Three Secret Poems* (1966), influenced by the Book of Revelation (having earlier rendered this, and The Song of Songs, into Modern Greek), and the former leftist Nikos Karouzos frequently deferred to religious themes.

interior one of alienation, despair and loss experienced amongst daily affairs and intimate relationships, often in works that are increasingly indirect and allusive as well as shorter in length (the first short prose-poems appear in the 1958–64 collection).

During this time Leivaditis worked as a literary critic for the newspaper, *Avghi* (*Dawn*), and also contributed to a number of other projects. In October 1961, for instance, he took part in a concert tour through the provinces with the composer Mikis Theodorakis, where during intermissions Leivaditis would read his poetry and engage with the audience. The same year Leivaditis co-wrote (with Kostas Kotzias) the screenplay, and contributed the lyrics for the songs (with music by Theodorakis), for the film 'The Suburb of Dreams' directed by Alekos Alexandrakis (1928–2005) — a landmark in neorealist Greek cinema.[1] Over the period 1962–66 Leivaditis also worked for the periodical *Epitheorisi Technis*, contributing literary and political articles, and in 1966 he published a collection of Kafkaesque short stories, entitled *The Pendulum*.

But all this activity was to come to an abrupt end on 21 April 1967 when, after a period of political instability, a military junta led by the Colonels (George Papadopoulos foremost among them) seized power and imposed martial law. Almost immediately thousands of people found themselves on the 'wanted' list — usually those with leftist sympathies, including Ritsos, Theodorakis, and the politician (and later Prime Minister) Andreas Papandreou — and were rounded up and taken to jail. Another repressive measure employed by the regime was censorship. During April 1967–

[1] Vrasidas Karalis, in *A History of Greek Cinema* (New York: Continuum, 2012), highlights the film's 'stark realism and bleak atmosphere and its depiction of the poverty and squalor dominating the Greek capital [Athens],' and judges it to be 'one of the best expressions of neorealism and one of the least recognized films of Greek cinema' (p. 107).

November 1969, when the dictatorship enforced 'preventive' censorship (that is, censorship of a work before it is made public), there was an unspoken agreement amongst nearly all Greek writers not to publish, and Leivaditis adhered to this in not publishing work of his own. After the dictatorship shut down the *Avghi* newspaper, Leivaditis found himself unemployed and also distressed to see his wife trying to make ends meet through her work as a seamstress. Luckily, Leivaditis was offered a job by friends who invited him to adapt and summarize literary classics for a variety of lowbrow periodicals. Leivaditis eagerly took this on, though given his communist background he had to write under a pseudonym, using the name 'A. Rokos'.

By late 1973 the Colonels' regime was in crisis. Following the occupation of the Athens Polytechnic by students in November 1973 and its brutal suppression by the regime, a coup was mounted by the army, led by Brigadier Ioannidis. Although Papadopoulos was deposed, the repressive measures continued and even intensified. Democracy would not be reinstated until July 1974, when Constantine Karamanlis was enthusiastically welcomed back from exile to reestablish democratic rule in Greece. The restoration of political order in Greece, followed by the decline of communism in Eastern Europe and the USSR, mirrored a further change in Leivaditis's career as he withdrew from political activity and took a more introspective and metaphysical direction.

In this third and final phase of Leivaditis's work, which begins with the publication of *Night Visitor* in 1972, the existential element becomes most intense as the poet's battles are now waged not against the forces of fascism, but against the threat of nihilism. As he put it in the prose-poem, 'Lamp':

> *Each time I begin to speak, I know that I'll say nothing: words will betray me, time will bypass me, the others will stand indifferent outside the house. Until, finally, I will*

be nothing other than someone who, holding a lamp,
would go from room to room
lighting the oblivion.[1]

The backdrop in these later works is frequently dark, desolate and oppressive, and the scenes are ones of violence, death and suicide (usually in the form of hanging) played out by often nameless characters who are ugly, mute, blind or debilitated in some way, or even dead but still hauntingly present. In the midst of this the poet becomes increasingly preoccupied ('obsessed' might be a better descriptor) with the question of the meaning of existence — a journey marked by melancholic loneliness, displacing the previous sense of communal or comradely struggle.

Night Visitor was followed in 1974 by *Dark Deed*, and in 1975 by *The Three* (a dialogue set in an asylum, where the third character 'is forbidden to speak') and *The Devil with the Candlestick*. His poetic narrative, *The Violin for the One-Armed Player* (1976), was runner-up in the State Poetry Prize, and in 1977 he published a lengthy volume of prose-poems entitled *Discovery*. His subsequent collection, *Handbook for Euthanasia*, was published in 1979 and won the State Poetry Prize. During this time Leivaditis also wrote the lyrics for various songs by Theodorakis, and Theodorakis too would set to music poems by Leivaditis (as he had done with poems by Seferis, Ritsos and Elytis) and in the process introduced his work to a much larger audience than before.

At the age of 61, and in declining health, Leivaditis published the work here translated: *The Blind Man with the Lamp* (1983). Two more works followed: *Violets for a Season* (1985) and *A Small Book for Big Dreams* (1987). On 30 October 1988, early on Sunday morning, Leivaditis died,

[1] Leivaditis, 'Lamp', *Handbook for Euthanasia*, in *Poetry, vol. 3: 1979–1990*, p. 74.

xxii

aged 66, at the General State Hospital in Athens from an abdominal aortic aneurism. Fittingly, he was accorded a state funeral. A final collection, *Autumn Manuscripts*, was published posthumously in 1990. His writings have been brought together in three volumes, published by Kedros, spanning in total nearly 1,400 pages.

* * *

The Blind Man with the Lamp, as mentioned earlier, belongs to the third and last phase of Leivaditis's output. The book is divided into four sections: the volume begins with 'Laurels for the Defeated', a collection of 36 short prose-poems; this is followed by twelve prayer-like 'Conversations' addressed to the Lord; the religious character of the work is continued with a short section entitled 'Brother Jesus', consisting of four brief passages, reminiscent of the Gospels, and given the titles of 'Annunciation', 'The birth', 'The burial' and 'The ascension'; and the book concludes with another long series of prose-poems, 44 in all, grouped under the heading 'Up All Night'.

My intention is not to provide a detailed analysis of the book but to introduce some of its themes and techniques as a way of motivating the reader to take up and indeed contemplate this masterful collection. Although a late work, many of the characteristics of Leivaditis's earlier writings reappear here, including the everyday or conversational tone of speech (Leivaditis invariably steers clear of the purist or *katharevousa* variety of Greek), corresponding to the humble and familiar settings of the poems (e.g., a living room, a coffee-house, a street corner); the abundant use of ellipses, unanswered or rhetorical questions, and paradoxical sequences and surrealist imagery (a classic example: 'I believe in beautiful birds which fly out from the most bitter books,' from 'Credo'); and also a special affinity for the outcasts of society: the blind, the beggars, the anarchists, the mentally ill — 'those poor and mad souls who imagined themselves to be birds, ladders or trees,' as Leivaditis wonderfully puts it in 'Entry Prohibited'. But by this stage, in 1983, important differences in his writing style had emerged. The epic stature of his earlier writings came to be replaced by short, compact and even aphoristic poems, sometimes only a line or two long. And the lyrical form of his previous work was to give way to poems that tend more towards prose and narrative.

The most significant change, however, concerns the mood and substance of the poems. Leivaditis's previous commitment to the politics of the Left had by now been transformed into, though not entirely supplanted by, a broader and deeper quest of existential and religious proportions, thus justifying the appellation given him of 'heretic of the Left'.[1] Although retaining his always strong social conscience, he had now embarked upon a passionate search for metaphysical meaning after what he regarded as the betrayal of his youthful hopes for creating a more just world here on earth.[2] The extent of the ground Leivaditis had traversed is nicely captured in two identically titled poems, 'Comradely Song'. In its first and lengthier incarnation, in the 1956 collection *The Man with the Drum*, the poem is a veritable eulogy to the Volga river as a symbol of the virtues and sacrifices of the workers and

[1] It is clear from his later writings that Leivaditis remained to the end sympathetic at least to the Left. To take just one example: in the posthumously published prose-poem, 'Histories', he wrote: 'On that night I was going down a side street when I noticed a man being harassed by the police. He was middle-aged with a small beard. "What's your name?" they asked him. He was completely silent. "Leave him!", I said, "I paid with my soul for him. His name is Lenin".' (Leivaditis, *Poetry, vol. 3: 1979–1990*, p. 498)

[2] I would venture that a similar trajectory can be identified in Kazant - zakis, who in the last decade of his life wrote the bulk of his novels and was moving away from both the communism and the heroic nihilism of his past to a view of the world more in keeping with mystical strands of Christianity.

soldiers of the Soviet Union.[1] But by 1983, the version included in the present translation has taken on a far more mournful, if not ironical, character. The poet's days are best 'passed over in silence' and the nights, where the stars no longer 'refute futility', are ones 'which I want to forget'. The 'old, comradely song' the poet whistles on his highway journey has now become only so much whistling in the wind.

The Blind Man with the Lamp gives powerful voice to the elegiac remembrance of the past and the concomitant desire for something wholly (and holy) Other. Memories of the battles and personalities of bygone days, imbued with feelings of loss and mourning, are portrayed so intimately that we almost believe that they are our very own. The nostalgia for 'the great days we lived through' ('Rain') is great and painful: we live 'with our watches stopped at another time' ('Soft Music'), and 'at night a gunshot from the past would suddenly be heard and the nostalgia would kill me' ('The Great Sin'). That past, and the poet who still resides there, are barely remembered today, and so stories of 'my wartime adventures' are met with incredulous stares ('The Unknown Soldier'). The postwar generation have already become 'the forgotten ones' ('Findings'), living amongst 'withered leaves and uprisings' ('In Memoriam'). All that remains is their memory of lost causes and ideals, or 'broken dreams and dead music' ('Years of Fire'), 'that great error in which we took refuge' ('Choice') — referring, of course, to the utopias of communism.[2]

---

[1] In the original edition, the poem was dedicated to Stalin. In later reprints, the dedication was altered to: 'For the unknown dead in the USSR during the Second World War.'

[2] This scepticism towards Causes and ideologies is evident in much of Leivaditis's later work. In *Handbook for Euthanasia* he wrote: '...but how many questions in this world have answers / and honesty always begins there, where all other paths to salvation have come to an end' ('The Key to the Mystery', *Poetry, vol. 3*, p. 96). In a similar vein, he was to write some years later: 'I loved the ideals of humanity / but the birds always

These dreams have now turned into nightmares, keeping the poet up all night, as the last section of the collection is entitled. In 'The Dream', Leivaditis expresses in his inimitable way this nightmarish vision of the past, where the narrator awakes startled and sweating: 'But what if one night I don't wake up at the right moment?' As a consequence, the night and the falling of the night (in twilight) are regularly portrayed as ominous and menacing: 'the difficulties, however, would begin at night' ('True Stories!'). The poet's insomnia results not only from unfulfilled hopes and tragic scenes from the past, but also from a guilty and recriminating conscience ('Public Prosecutor', 'The Denial of Peter', 'Sleep'), even if the poet has been guilty only of 'a great innocence' ('Guilt').

The threat of despair and nothingness, where 'nothing will be rectified' (repeated twice in 'Findings') and 'oblivion always wins out' ('Report'), is not simply counteracted but fused and interconnected with a deep religious sensibility — and specifically a profound longing for the inscrutable Other, where 'there begins another world, an unknown world' ('Foretaste'). The poet goes on to ask: 'who has ever gone there? who has ever returned from there?' ('Foretaste'), but the horrendous evils of the twentieth century convince him that 'somewhere there must be a better world...' (conclusion to 'The ascension' in the 'Brother Jesus' series). This longing for the Other is often expressed in terms of an erotic desire for God, in tones reminiscent of the biblical Song of Songs: '...and I pray, uttering the name of God like a woman in love biting her handkerchief' ('Excerpt From a Future Poem'), and in the final line in 'Scenes from the Station' the poet confesses

flew further' (from *Small Book for Big Dreams*, in *Poetry, vol. 3*, p. 352). Again, from the same work: 'I remember one evening it was snowing, and as I was walking with my collars up through the desolate city I encountered old Marx, his biblical-like beard swaying in the wind. "Where are you going?" he asked me. "To the devil," I replied. "I'll come with you," he said.' (*Small Book for Big Dreams*, in *Poetry, vol. 3*, p. 405).

that he 'was hankering after God' (or, more literally: 'I was sick for God').

In an article on Leivaditis's 'sickness for God', the distinguished theatre critic Kostas Georgousopoulos identifies one of the possible precedents of Leivaditis's quest:

> Whoever decides to read the spiritual sufferings printed on the pages of Leivaditis's books will establish that this poet has perhaps unconsciously imitated the life of many saints, who began as haughty teachers, preachers, trumpeters and leaders, but at a critical juncture on the road they changed direction and journeyed using as their only compass their own struggle [τήν ἀγωνία τους] and not the Cause [τόν ἀγώνα].[1]

In a similar vein, the contemporary Greek poet Elias Kephalas has described Leivaditis's later work as a 'lyrical theology' which

> ...underscores Leivaditis's transcendence of every ideological prejudice and his definitive release from all forms of bondage, so that he could finally belong entirely to himself and in this way belong genuinely to all the world. The religious shudder which was to run untrammelled through his poetry underscores and highlights the greatest of all truths: the insignificance of humanity.[2]

This 'religious shudder' is apparent in the very prayerfulness of *The Blind Man with the Lamp*, especially in the section subtitled 'Conversations', where each of the twelve poems begins with 'Lord...', as though making an invocation or

[1] Kostas Georgousopoulos, 'One Hankering After God' [in Greek], *I Lexi*, vol. 130, November–December 1995, p. 739. This issue of *I Lexi* is dedicated to the work of Leivaditis.

[2] Elias Kephalas, 'The Religious Shudder in Tasos Leivaditis and Human Insignificance' [in Greek], *To Dendro*, no. 171–72, Autumn 2009, p. 46. This issue of *To Dendro* is dedicated to the work of Leivaditis.

appeal to God. Indeed, the entire volume gives the impression of a single, long prayer, the creator conversing with his Creator, but a conversation spontaneously spoken from an anguished heart rather than one carefully crafted and edited on paper. As one commentator put it, referring to the 'Conversations' and 'Brother Jesus' sections of the work, 'readers may ask themselves whether these have been written by a church hymnographer given that they exude the musicality and evocativeness of hymns.'[1] This effect is aided by Leivaditis's paratactic manner of writing: a continuous prose-like style, created in part by the sparse use of periods within each poem (something I have sought in my translation to reproduce by the use of hyphens). We could therefore say that Leivaditis's language and style elicit and enact, and not merely describe or recount, a particular way of relating to God — one that does not reduce God to a fact or dogma, but sees in God the possibility of endless questioning and exploration. As the French-Jewish writer, Edmond Jabès (whose work bears many similarities with Leivaditis's), stated: 'God is a questioning of God.'[2]

The questioning and searching is endless because God himself is infinite and inexhaustible. Indebted to the mystical or apophatic tradition of Orthodox theology (according to which God is ineffable, unnameable and unknowable), Leivaditis constantly emphasizes the divine darkness and hiddenness and hence the inadequacy of our words in the face of this mystery: 'all speech wounds you' ('Conversations 2'). Our language to and about God therefore requires nothing less than a transfiguration, and so the poet asks the Lord to 'give to my words something of that great ineffability /

[1] Alexandra Bouphea, 'The Search for God in the Work of Tasos Leivaditis's [in Greek], *Diavazo*, no. 228, 13 December 1989, p.78. This issue includes a series of articles dedicated to the writings of Leivaditis.

[2] Edmond Jabès, *The Book of Questions, volume 1*, trans. Rosmarie Waldrop (Hanover, NH: Wesleyan University Press, 1991), p. 138.

which makes you silent' ('Conversations 8'). But Leivaditis's apophaticism is a generalized one, applying as much to the earthly as to the divine. This is Leivaditis's 'learned ignorance' regarding the elusiveness and obscurity of life itself, reflected in the recurring image of blindness and in the abstruse and paradoxical quality of many of the poems. As he was to write in his posthumously published *Autumn Manuscripts*: 'Every time they would speak to me about God, I never believed them. But later when I remained alone in the silence, I came to understand both God and his work.'[1] However, this clarity is diminished as soon as the sign, whether verbal or not, appears: 'One morning a bird sat on the opposite tree and whistled something. / O, if only I could understand what it was saying to me, perhaps I could have found the meaning of the universe!'[2]

Radical transcendence, therefore, is not only the province of God but is also our own vocation: 'in order to enter the mystery / they must leave behind their own selves' ('Entry Prohibited'). Paradoxically, it is only through such self-transcendence that we find, or perhaps regain, our true selves and our true place. Prior to that, our being is experienced as foreign and strange, an unsettling not-being-at-home, or what Heidegger called *unheimlichkeit* to express the essential homelessness of the human being. For Leivaditis, 'our real life is elsewhere and here we wander about lost' ('Quests'), and it is the dead who provide us with the 'sure route' home (from 'Sure Route', which Leivaditis dedicated to his three brothers). Just as for Socrates 'true philosophers make dying

---

[1] Leivaditis, 'The Constellation of Leo', *Autumn Manuscripts*, in *Poetry, vol. 3*, p. 442.

[2] Leivaditis, 'The Bird with the Truth', *Autumn Manuscripts*, in *Poetry, vol. 3*, p. 418. In the same volume, Leivaditis writes: 'How incomprehensible it is to live' ('Time', *Autumn Manuscripts*, p. 480), and 'Each of us has a great secret and we will depart without finding out what it is / neither we, nor anyone else' ('Thought at Twilight', *Autumn Manuscripts*, p. 545).

their profession' (*Phaedo* 67e), so for Leivaditis poetry 'is another form of dying' ('Unknown Debts') and it is the poet who follows the lead of his dead and thus finds his way back home. It is therefore no surprise to see the question of location and dislocation brilliantly resolved towards the end of the book, in the space of a few lines:

A QUESTION OF LOCATION

In the evenings friends go looking for me in the coffee-houses, where they find a glass of cognac emptying slowly slowly on its own —
> *but what else was I to do given that I existed always on the other side of life.*

N. N. Trakakis
Melbourne, Australia
January 2014

THE

BLIND MAN

WITH THE

LAMP

LAURELS

FOR THE

DEFEATED

THE BLIND MAN WITH THE LAMP

IT WAS NIGHT and I had made the greatest decision of the century — I would save humanity — but how? — as thousands of thoughts were tormenting me I heard footsteps, opened the door and beheld the blind man from the opposite room walking down the hallway and holding a lamp — he was about to go down the stairs — 'What is he doing with the lamp?', I asked myself and suddenly an idea flashed through my mind — I found the answer — 'My dear brother,' I said to him, 'God has sent you,'

and with zeal we both got down to work ...

I MEAN that each night I had to go for broke, and of course without anyone being on the other side of the table — no-one? we are a joke — opposite me over there, every night, stands God — I try to get away from him — I come up with ruses, mortal sins, hideous thoughts, but He claims me whole — I am enraged that I can't find any escape, any way out ...

Until it begins to dawn. I open the window, and without meaning to I smile. God, one more time, has beaten me with his brand new day.

COMRADELY SONG

I COME from days which must be passed over in silence, from nights which I want to forget — I walked trembling in the bustle of the big cities — I saw the great clocks of the churches entering into alliance with the devil — I saw the poor walking quietly on the road like Christ on the waters — popular uprisings granted me royal afternoons, but at night I was endangered in a desolate garden.

He who opened the door so as to sleep did not see the stars refuting futility — those who buried their dead do not know what remembrance means —

humble men, who awoke with a straw caught in their hair, as though they had just been glorified somewhere else,

and I would take to the highway whistling: 'O old, comradely song.'

From that moment (where all of you will find yourselves at some point), I realized that there is no other solution — I would therefore go around at night rattling letterboxes along the streets — they owe me an answer — besides, it is dishonourable when you don't have anything to eat to be going around buying revolvers to get confessions — or how could you not cry for him who has to wait for the following September? — and so, despite all my precautions they managed to succeed — as I turned the corner they captured me and put someone else in my place — 'Help!', I shouted — my voice was heard from afar — 'At least my dead will recognize me,' I thought and ran to the station

and slowly slowly it grew dark and the city was disappearing into an inconceivable abyss —

and I was hankering after God.

Since then I like to occupy myself with public affairs, or else I migrate to a more beautiful truth — but why should I not be honest: it was simply a long hospital ward — 'No, doctor,' I told him, 'I am not an alcoholic — all the wine I used to drink was drunk by the demon' — and only an old man at the far end of the corridor would look at me compassionately — he may well have been my uncle (relationships are so inexplicable) — finally they discharged me — where could I go? — I stood by the edge of the road besides piles of rubbish and I was overtaken by the boundless joy that I am not alone — from then on I fulfil my old dream: I drive the tip of my umbrella into the earth and I converse with the seasons, or else I sit on the floor waiting for a nameless visit

precisely because for years now the door has been locked.

A GREAT PAST

AND NOW that we have finally extricated ourselves from great words, exploits, dreams, it is time to return to our lives — but it is in vain — the layout of the city has changed — where is the road where we fell in love with each other when we were young? where did the wind go which scattered so many comrades? does the world still exist? — now old songs become entangled in our language — no-one understands us and only the children fathom much, but they grow up quickly and the birds fly so that they may not remember — such a past and nothing remains except for some ashes, where bent over at night we design flags, stars, hills, horses, and amongst them the regret that we didn't give it our all

in this way liberating bygone pledges and the most beautiful gestures of the future.

CARE

THE SILENCE was absolute — I mean for others, because I always had at hand the last gunshots (from an uprising now long gone) — besides I'm a human being too, and I need to have some cares: a dream or a mother or even some sudden contempt which makes you forget everything, like the scent of the cypress trees at night

which consoles you as regards futility itself.

PROLOGUE TO ETERNITY

SOMEDAY I will return. I am the only heir.
And my dwelling lies wherever I look.

SOFT MUSIC

IN THE END there was not a single night when I would not write on the frosted window a few words for us as well — the words would be quickly erased — who remembers us? — many companions died, others disappeared even more definitively — those of us who survived walk on the side, with our watches stopped at another time (that's why we age so painfully) — only occasionally as we awkwardly turn our hats soft music can be heard from old worn-out exploits — we are in any case quite proud in order that we may be heard more vividly. Silence.

We have been besmirched by men but our beauty will be preserved by the anonymity of History.

FORESIGHT

W E LIVED forgotten and unknown — columns from temples in ruins — black porticoes —

old, furrowed land which promised only an eternal sleep —

and O wise foresight of the children who from early on make friends with the soil.

HISTORY LESSON

W RETCHED WE ARE, fighting by night with dreams and by day with legends — then come delusions, disdain, slaughtered animals, fever. And I wonder: in which direction are the inverted eyes of the dead looking?

In this way we always had an escape route...

GOOD NEWS

I WAS very tired, crippled by a mysterious accident which happened or was going to happen sometime (dates usually deceive) — so I ran to save humanity and I would trample on my neighbours — I wrote my name on the walls in the hope that they would remember me and later I returned and wiped it off so that I don't have anywhere to lean on — or, I gave a few coins away to the poor: charity does good, it exercises one's arm — truly, when I recall that time of my life I prefer to sleep, but how could I? — the devil comes and demands the overdue rent — I go, then, to the hospital, but I know too much and they kick me out — and so I go to a run-down house and for a small fee I lie down on the bed and wait for news from Babylon...

JUSTICE

I REMEMBER that dishevelled woman who would swear at me — a yellow decayed tooth would protrude from her mouth. 'She must have just cause,' I thought.

Otherwise what was the point of it?

THE DREAM

Every night the same bizarre dream. It's as though they enter through the walls — you have no time to put up a defence — they chase one man up the avenue — they can't reach him with their axes, which clank dreadfully on the asphalt — they then pin him with a bayonet — no-one knows how they got hold of it — afterwards someone appears on horseback — 'It must be his soul,' I think to myself — the other man they drown inside a shop — to frighten me, of course, they open the door a little and show me his lifeless hand — before me came the turn of the girl — 'Stay there, close to the world,' I tell her, 'perhaps they'll get scared' — practically a child, but they take no pity on her — 'Is there no-one here?', I shout. 'They're killing us!' — and suddenly they appear beside me — I cry out in fear, 'Help!', and I awake drenched in sweat.

But what if one night I don't wake up at the right moment?

PREOCCUPATIONS

Perhaps I made a mistake by not writing it down immediately, but how could it be made believable? — from then on I have avoided every kind of occupation — no-one knows what dangers are hidden in ordinary things — out of all my acquaintances I prefer a friendship that is imaginary, such as that with Miss Glykeria: whenever I need her she is here, whereas so many of my friends have gone for good — or I stand outside second-hand shops and I look at the old sewing machines which sad women leant on to weep — 'What, after all, do you want from me?' I shouted and I continued to cut out with scissors great dreams from paper, but they insisted: This dreamy look — what did you want with it? And the birds — why do they instantly recognize you? And, most importantly, what to preoccupy myself with given that the creation of the world had already been completed?

PUBLIC PROSECUTOR

You can deal with anything: sadness, affliction, even shattered dreams.

But how can you be defended from that imaginary person who makes accusations against you in an empty room at the moment when you are going down the stairs.

LEARNING

OCCASIONALLY as you are on your way home at night, the moment you pass by the third lamp post (strange, but exactly there), it is as though you are passing in front of your very own misfortune — you stand dumbfounded, you try to understand, but all is shrouded in darkness and above all your past — who were you? — the nights are long, and each morning you have to learn about life from scratch — what's the point, then, of going to Vladivostok in order to be humiliated? — I approach the first man I chance upon, that way I get away with not paying for a ticket — besides I too had my principles, first: I would not decide anything without looking at my watch, something which would often embroil me in mysterious affairs, and second: how could I work, you idiots, when I adored my mother?

And I spent an entire lifetime with eyes glued to the window — that's how I know devastation from up close.

TWILIGHT

IF I LOST my life it is because I always had another age apart from the real one and now long since I've mixed them up — I don't know if I am at the end or the beginning, if I must go or return, and what road to take and where to go — in any case it has gone dark

and the dogs are barking, stopping the passers-by at the borders of the inexpressible.

SECRET WORKS

Usually they look at me with derision as I sit on the doorstep for hours — many indeed laugh ostentatiously — 'idle', they say — they don't know that all the while I am giving out great handshakes to the anarchists, Christmas cards to the birds and distant horizons to those who are running late.

To your health then! Each day is our best day.

THE DECEPTIONS OF THE CALENDAR

I NEVER would have imagined that so many days go to make up so short a life.

TRUE CAUSES

AND THOSE who collect the cast-offs of the world do so not to wear them,

but simply to cover the lamp at night, so that they can forgive.

IMMORTAL PLATITUDES

THE DAYDREAMERS return tired (from where?) — in their eyes the suburbs have been flooded;

in the asylum they measure endurance with their liceand the magnitude of the day with their tears;

suddenly the guard grabs me by the neck, I am taken aback and then the most beautiful music is heard —

our aged continent travels like a plank of wood from an old shipwreck.

NEVERTHELESS, no-one could yet predict the end — it was, as I recall, dusk, a time that is pledged to God and bodes the executioner — in any case I was troubled also by the enigma of my birth — I mean to say that my parents were mortal, whereas I had other aspirations — and the spout, like a slit throat, would sing in autumn — or, who has not burned their hands in the fire of this world? — but one will wonder, will they not?, why I would sleep with my arms around the very phonebook which was betraying my principles — ah! this too was a pledge for a little less loneliness, some booty from the everlasting anonymity — until day would break

and a new sorrow would come to save me from the previous one.

HE WAS PECULIAR and perhaps that's why he could pass through an entire city without being harmed
making those small concessions which mothers make to dreams and the defeated to credulity.

ENTRY PROHIBITED

Entry was prohibited, except to those poor and mad souls who imagined themselves to be birds, ladders or trees — vaguely divining that in order to enter the mystery they must leave behind their own selves.

IN MEMORIAM

ONE DAY we will receive a letter, it will be from another era — perplexed, we will leave it on the table — we will think to ourselves how much we are still strangers — words will have become spectres — on the street you will sometimes find a visiting-card, but we will have no memory, the coffee-houses will be empty like landscapes of the beyond — and only I, the madman, will then get up and shout: 'Comrades!', as though I were answering this endless silence...

The calendar will show that it's October — with its withered leaves and uprisings.

THE MYSTERIOUS QUALITIES OF MONEY

IN THE EVENING, as it is getting dark, if you have nothing better to do, leave a small coin outside your window — at any place in the city.

You will understand immediately what I'm getting at.

UNKNOWN TRIAL

I AM USUALLY anxious as night falls — it is the time when the undergarment seamstresses are in danger on the road — they have just returned from holy Russia, where they had sewn the shrouds of great eras — I run to rescue them — at the law court where I testify they listen to me in stupefaction — as a sign of appreciation I hold an umbrella which I open only at times of reverie — 'A bit of honesty!', I shouted — they laughed.

Finally I am sentenced — I am executed — but persistent as I am, I prepare a new plan of escape — only I lack, as always, a quiet afternoon and a small final hope...

RESEMBLANCES

L<small>IFE</small>, unlike children, has no pity, and unlike poetry it has no friendships. And the world resembles my mother: beloved
 and lost forever.

AS NIGHT FALLS

D<small>EEP DOWN</small> there is always a hidden and inscrutable impulse, from old farewells, from distant silences in cold rooms

while as night falls panic again breaks out —

evil is incurable, and the roof of the house a dreadful menace

for those who forget.

THE CITY

I WALK HUNCHED — I am a stranger in this city — but the sour smell coming from the public toilets strangely impels me — one of my delights are the Observatories — at least they have heating — and if the clerk had paid attention to my face he would have discerned many future floods — in short, a miserable afternoon, the kind you'd want to hang yourself — the screams had indeed stopped — the protest march had just finished and the police officers were erasing an entire revolution that was written on the walls...

A CHILLY DAY

That morning I awoke with an unbearable sorrow because I had never spoken about heliotropes — it was strange, if not also contemptible — I looked in the rooms, I searched the hallway, I went to the basement: 'How did my childhood years fit in here?' I asked myself — I smiled — 'I must've been somewhere else' — and I remembered mother all alone in the room in the evenings — she would wear that old hat with the feathers as though she wanted to show that everything had finished —

I sat exhausted on the stairs — then the doorbell rang — I went to open the door — it was once again the man with the axe — 'You scum!' I said to him. 'What are you playing at? I was simply thinking of you.' And he replied: 'Do you think you will be spared?'

CREDO

I BELIEVE in broken watches because I can spit on them
without fear

I believe in the five continents because of their pretty colours
on the map

I believe in empty rooms which, when you unlock them, you
sometimes find your own self

I believe in madmen at the time when they are praying and
in apple trees at night when they are thinking

I believe in the small and worn keepsakes of my mother and
in the immaculate conception of the Virgin

I believe in the voice of the umbrella merchant which is an
entirely wasted youth

I believe in beautiful birds which fly out from the most bitter
books

I believe in the friend you suddenly meet inside a fairy tale

I believe in the unbelievable which is our truest history

I believe in the moon when it falls in the well so that the back
of the rickety child may be hidden from view as he
bends down to look at it

I believe in dogs which, when they bark, lift up their heads as
though they see someone passing by from on high...

RAIN

ONE NIGHT we will create a great idea, but we mustn't tell it to anyone (this is the sole justice) — afterwards we will take to the streets — it will be raining and rain too has its own private life, whereas we had no such thing — given that we are mortal and since the heavens are aware of our innocence we will hang around a pharmacy — finally, as day breaks, we will knock on the door of our house, but no-one will recognize us — it is incredible, just like the great days we lived through. Goodbye, then. Let's open our umbrellas and let's hurriedly leave behind

the end of an era.

FORETASTE

A LITTLE FURTHER from the light cast by the lamp there begins another world, an unknown world — who has ever gone there? who has ever returned from there? — and then there are the nights — ah! how many adventures there are in dreams, so many that your life becomes insignificant (and hence dangerous) — then night falls and that old familial rain begins again, just like the time when mother would not let me go out and we would play together in the room: I would hide from her and she would search and search for me, but would not be able to find me — 'Where are you?' she would then shout, frightened,

for I had already become submerged in all my future sorrows.

WE ARE THOSE who have been on their way for centuries — we never had a place of our own — where are we going? where are we coming from? On occasion we stay somewhere for a while, but Fate quickly remembers us again and we leave.

And only on occasion, at the time when dusk falls and the few violets shudder amongst the hedges, we are overwhelmed by a strange awe, a feeling as though we are returning to the place from which we had been forever banished.

Or perhaps the twilight is our only homeland...

CONVERSATIONS

I

LORD, let me come near you. Perhaps with my great poverty,
     my smallness, my great remorse, I could comfort
     you a little
during those nights when I hear you cry. Because so much
     perfection has become by now a great tribulation.

2

LORD, only in silence do we feel you. All speech wounds
you.
And our words are your injuries from which, together with
your blood,
there drips a bit of infinity.

3

LORD, you are our daily bread, our great longing to return
  — where?
You are the womb which will give birth to us by means of our
  death.
Amen.

4

LORD, you are hidden behind so many enigmas, shadows,
dark sayings — how am I to find you?
But there are moments when I recognize you: a sudden excess
in my heart betrays you.

5

LORD, what would I do without you? I am the vacant room
and you are the great guest who has deigned to visit it.
Lord, what would you do without me? You are the great silent
harp and I am the ephemeral hand which awakens your
melodies.

6

LORD, we have been living together for centuries in the same room, but I can't see your face.

Yet I sometimes hear you walking heavily inside my words, eager to surmount the limits of this world.

7

Lᴏʀᴅ, you are the great infinity that we breathe, the endless
   path that we travel on.
You are the indescribable silence that we hear within us and
   through which we speak — so that we may not die
   from fright.

8

LORD, we both live in the dark, the one cannot see the other
     — but stretch out your hand and I will find it, let me
     talk to you and you will hear me,
only give to my words something of that great ineffability
     which makes you silent.

9

LORD, I searched for you everywhere: in the glories of the
      earth and the heavens, in the splendour of the great
      cities, at the crossroads of the ages —
while you would meekly and quietly spend the night in my
      most indefinable reverie.

10

LORD, my sin turned out to be that I wished to resolve your
    paradox, to penetrate your mystery
and in this way I deceived myself, the fool —for I am your
    great secret.

I I

LORD, you are the eternal traveller who at one moment sank
    next to the hedge to go to sleep
and I am the fleeting dream which keeps you company in
    your slumber.

Lord, let's not wake up just yet — it's early.

12

LORD, from you everything begins. And to you everything
   will come to be brought to completion.
And spring is nothing more than your nostalgia for those few
   hours you lived on earth.

BROTHER

JESUS

...I BELIEVE in the diffident and awkward steps of the humble and in Christ who crosses History...

HE WAS, no doubt, always a little strange — he lived in the room next door — but that night he came out on the street holding a lamp — 'What are you looking for?' I asked him — 'The Mother of God' he said to me — in that incomprehensible language of those

who give meaning to an entire era.

On another night I heard him crying next-door. I knocked on the door and went in. He showed me a small wooden cross on top of the bedside table. 'You see,' he said to me, 'compassion is born.' I then bowed my head and I too cried,

for centuries and centuries would go by and we would not have anything more beautiful to say than that.

H<small>E DIED</small> after a few days. We buried him at the edge of an old cemetery — two men in all and a stray dog passing by which had stopped to watch us. It was raining.

That's why, every time I now see a dog, I know wherein lies Paradise.

MONTHS went by. The room next door remained vacant. Until a new tenant arrived. I never saw his face — I would only hear, day and night, his unceasing pacing in the room. 'He must be travelling very far,' I thought. Finally, one night the pacing stopped. 'At last he has arrived,' I said to myself with relief.

The next morning I found out that he had left — because, my God, somewhere there must be a better world...

UP

ALL NIGHT

SANCTITY

THE CALENDAR imperturbable on the wall — some day of the month and the saints are silent, ashen and sinless, marked only by their first names, just as they were called by their mothers.

Lord, no-one wanted to grow up.

THE DENIAL OF PETER

I DON'T KNOW how it happened or whether it happened in the way told by the Evangelist — at any rate I was frightened, my tunic you might say hung empty, so much had I lost myself in fear. Three times I denied my God. And when the cock crowed I leant against the wall and cried. 'Lord, we are human,' I whispered. And then I realized that I had been forgiven. The Lord, as he was departing, left with me on earth

the first memory of his infinite mercy.

IT WAS a strange adventure — they had arrested me for unknown reasons — 'It's him! It's him!' they shouted — I naturally raised objections: 'But I was sleeping at that time,' I said to them — 'That's exactly why!' — a whole crowd had come together — they had even brought false witnesses who insisted: 'It's him!' — O my Lord and God, how could they have known me? I had never seen them before — 'Not even in your dreams?' they would ask — what could you say in reply? how could you save yourself from this savage and uncomprehending world? — I took off all my clothes and threw them at their feet: 'I have always stood naked before God!' I shouted.

By then night had fallen and many other things transpired to magnify my despair...

And my journey continued — I mean to say that I often walked along the train tracks on my own — where was I going? (I never found out) — the difficulties, however, would begin at night — I had to exchange letters, but with whom? I had no-one — and so I passionately devoted myself to walking, something which if you've never done you have yet to learn anything about the human condition — that is why our entire civilization is going under with the cobblers singing the requiem — besides there was also Teresa, always affable (like all those who are afraid) — her dress would fall like a sigh, but I was insatiable and would call her Eleonora — she in turn would cry and ask for a true story — because tell me who hasn't opened a door or a window without receiving the false impression

that this world exists . . .

DESCRIPTIONS

Rooms where we lived, but never learned their secrets
histories unforeseen by conjurors and other beleaguered souls
postcards of slaughterhouses for greater awareness
prison cells clothed in words for the years to go by
public toilets where perversion babbles childishly
an infancy full of marvellous flies
a Christian hymn for myself and those like me
a net made of sky on which madmen throw the most beautiful
      birds
or someone who hung himself from a wild pear tree and from
      its height leaped beyond futility.

So I was sitting on my own in the room and I suffered terribly, because deep down I am a nobody — night was falling and the city groaned like a dying dog underneath the bridges — but why does the rain always speak to us of some inescapable journey? — and these men on the street and in the coffee-house are complete strangers, and yet they remind you of something — where have you met them before? — perhaps amongst childhood fantasies or behind the curtains on very sad evenings —

many years then went by, life changed and only I insisted on passing the winter with old newspapers under my jacket (thus I got to know the news up close) — and at times I wanted to kill myself, so much would everything suddenly become beautiful — but faraway could be heard the rustling of eternity, and even further away father's coughing from bygone days...

OLD FRIENDSHIPS

AND DON'T WORRY about it — it's simple: cross your hands on top of the table and it will come on its own.

The mystery recognizes you even if you don't remember it.

GUILT

I HAVE to confess: I lived recklessly, and that's precisely why I loved the world — but why did I feel like a stranger? — my whole life seemed distant as though I were reading it in a book, with someone else turning the pages — I barely remember a few deserted roads, some harsh words and the doors hurriedly closed each time we had visitors (so that they would not see the abandonment in which the house was slowly sinking) — finally, surrounded by so many angels, how could one make a living? — a nostalgia for something we lost even before we were born

and at night I would kneel down on some deserted side street and I would look at the stars in despair — 'Where can I go?' I would ask — one night some friends appeared — embarrassed that I was knelt down, I made out that I was looking for something — 'Those damned matches!' I said loudly — if the area were lighted they would have seen that my face had turned bright red,

guilty of a great innocence.

THOUGHTS

THE DEAD leave behind an entire eternity unspent
lovers are lost in the night in the mystery of oneness
and those who triumphed quickly are lost forever...

THE UNKNOWN SOLDIER

Appearances often deceive, people are easily fooled — perhaps because they need to be, such is the difficulty of life — and so I too would be mocked whenever I would tell them about my wartime adventures, for the simple and base reason that from childhood I was stuck in a wheelchair — 'So where did you fight?' they would sarcastically ask — then one night there was a knock on the door — they opened it, and it was an old man with a long biblical-like beard — 'I was a station master in Kiev many years ago,' he said, 'and I have brought the army jacket you had left behind' — I looked at the others triumphantly — they were all speechless — I then bent over and kissed the hand of this old man who had traversed so much time and so many lost glories, to come here to remind us that we still exist...

ANNA THE ANARCHIST

How the story of my acquaintance with Anna began and ended was something I never quite understood — a girl of unparalleled beauty as well as anarchic — the judges would absent-mindedly draw trees on paper, but when her defence began it was like a wind had suddenly bent those trees over — the judges were startled, and when the sentence of 'Death' was delivered Anna smiled and unbuttoned her blouse a little, as though she were returning finally to her ownmost way of life ...

AFTERNOON INCIDENT

W E WERE SITTING in the garden when a woman we did not know stopped and stood outside the fence — she had carried herself as though she were about to climb some stairs and then suddenly changed her mind — 'Can you give me some water?' she said in a tranquil voice, and she would have had to endure much to have acquired a voice like that — afterwards, as she was giving us back the glass, on which traces of the sunset were reflected, her thin hand was wavering and trembling somewhat, as though she were trying to touch something we could not see. The glass fell and broke. 'Please forgive me,' she said, 'I am blind.'

And her gaze was fixed a little above us, onto fate itself.

WAITING

He was a pale young man — he was sitting on the pavement in the middle of winter, and he was cold. 'What are you waiting for?' I asked him. 'The next century,' he replied.

And snow was falling quietly quietly, as though on top of a grave.

APPEARANCES DECEIVE

'I AM a keeper of keys,' he would say, and standing in the middle of the ward he would gesture as though he were opening a lock — he would strain his ears to listen to the trains passing by, and then once more he would make his gestures, signals — twenty years now in the asylum, and even the madmen laugh at him — 'You are nothing!' they would say to him, and he would cry.

One evening I approached him — 'I know,' I said to him, 'you are a keeper of keys' — he smiled — 'No,' he said to me, 'I do it for the others. I am a qualified doctor, just as my mother wanted.'

It was Christmas eve and the three Magi were still on their way — in the living room of her parents' house Mrs Koula had escaped the deluge and now, having grown old, she would pass on to me like a silent illness her lousy French — since then I have had an obsession for posthumous fame — so I would go to the shops and I would tell people about so many of my tribulations that the days began to grow weary — and other times I would lay the tablecloth nicely, even though I would not eat anything other than my own entrails — on one occasion, to be sure, I met an acquaintance on the street — 'I have good news,' he told me — 'What?' I said. 'Have the dead been resurrected?'

From then on I have been afraid of words. What's the point of even more disappointments?

UNEXPECTED SOLUTIONS

THE SUN set slowly slowly. And night time arrived.

Just like our very hands which kill off our most beautiful gestures.

REFLECTIONS

And when I no longer have any other way to make a living I'll take a big mirror and I'll stand at street corners, just like those with weighing machines or pamphlets with the lives of saints, and there for a few coins I'll let those passing by look at their reflections, that they may see for a moment within the depths of the mirror

the entire emptiness that follows us...

THE UNATTAINABLE

As FOR my relatives, I had no news from them since the time of the flood, even though I would sometimes happen to meet them in the hallway or the dining room, each one of us chasing after a little expiation or a name written in snow — and Uncle Ignatius, an elderly, ill and longtime tailor, would always sew stooped over next to the window, entangling the threads with the roads of the city — many lost their bearings as a result — but I stand undaunted at the station looking at the birds pecking at crumbs from lost journeys — it is wonderful although dangerous, like someone who all their life would cry while writing — they would write, and how much they suffered

would always remain outside.

DEPARTURE

And perhaps it was there that I discovered destiny — I mean to say that I too was young at one time and yet I handed back my inheritance so that it may be put to better use — I only kept my mother's armchair which I carried along all the windswept roads of this black century — 'Mother,' I would say, 'this world is not for us' — the platforms would shudder from the departures of old — I would sleep with thirty-two clocks in my dreams, suspicious like some historical personage —

and then all of a sudden, by the time I went down the steps, life passed by — we sat with Teresa at the bar opposite — 'I want them to remember me,' she said while crying — I ordered two more drinks — 'Let's drink,' I said to her, and I would think of our future journey: passengers of tombs for all eternity.

CHOICE

WE LED a quiet life, dignified and deprived — but that great error in which we took refuge, perhaps that's where one will find the roses

    which every night lay siege to our sleep.

A QUESTION OF MEMORY

THERE IS ALWAYS an old mortifying word which murderers seek to forget

but which those who die by their own hand had the power to recall again.

… WITHIN ME rain of biblical proportions, which I gave away to itinerant umbrella merchants — city planners sized me up but could not get to the bottom of me — traders weighed me but ended with a surplus as big as the world — they gave me some money so that my anxiety about it would rob me of my sleep — but I slept on the railway tracks so that I may travel to an unfulfilled dream — and I became a sleepwalker so that the unknown would not be left all alone at my door — and I became an icon so that I would remain silent in full knowledge — and when night fell I cried like the traveller who passed over the five oceans unscathed only suddenly to be shipwrecked on the alphabet.

O secret night! Receive me! I am an unarmed man like a vowel which incites a city — day will soon dawn — vine-growers whistle as they gather the miracles of the day and I pray, uttering the name of God like a woman in love biting her handkerchief — nothing more than a man of my time, inexplicable and vulnerable

O difficulties which take us further away…

YEARS OF FIRE

Behind the shutters dark scenes are being played out
those who had a vision for the future were lost so young —

we lived with broken dreams and dead music ...

ERAS

Sometimes, while it is quiet, the house suddenly rattles, the glasses tremble on top of the table, a picture on the wall is displaced — and at that time I think to myself there must be some people outside who are on their way

outside and on their way towards new eras.

QUESTS

In the end you were my only friend, even if you were a figment of my imagination — but what counts as imaginary when I owe you my most beautiful tears? — in any case our real life is elsewhere and here we wander about lost — only sometimes I stop and look at the depth of the sky, a depth which has much to tell you when you are finally as good as dead — and later I run around again searching like a madman, to find what? — to find what, when eternity has remained forever in the old family garden.

And as night fell I began to sing, because the song is the end, since everything began in the silence...

SURE ROUTE

In memory of my brothers
Dinos, Mimis and Alekos

Aᴎᴅ ʙᴇᴄᴀᴜsᴇ my economic situation was getting worse by the day, I started to become resourceful: I would, for example, go down to the basement where there was an old, broken clock — I would set it at the most critical hour and wait — and may the name of God be blessed, I was never wide of the mark — later, with pride, I would go to the tavern, where the steam from the pans would fill me with religious thoughts — the poor folk would be crammed together, drunkards with trampled hats and hackneyed words like the ages — until, at last, drunk, I would follow from behind one of my dead and in this way I would always find my home...

FINDINGS

Dreamers always stand to the side because only through
there will he pass
the poor to whom they give alms generously offer their own
selves
words grow in nights of forgetfulness
women iron the underclothes of strangers and then go to the
door and weep
and he who does a big round before going home, because he
does not yet want to acknowledge it — no, don't ask
me, nothing will be rectified
deserted children who quietly depart from childhood
carefree birds which go on leave for an entire year
statues too have their melancholic moments
poems — keys for madness or the sky
reputation — that slaughterhouse
I dream of a hospital for ill fairy tales, of swans in the hats of
the condemned, of laurels for the defeated
we the forgotten ones, for whom a smile suffices to pass
beyond the bounds of the world.
Goodbye, goodbye ... Nothing will be rectified ...

LIFE

Day departed wrapped up in the ephemeral clamour.
But in the evening the dreamer throws some salt on the stone
and calls upon his God.

SLEEP

Every night, around midnight, some people would enter my room, people I barely remembered: the ill with fiery eyes behind the windows of the hospitals, women at the doorstep with socks fallen down, dead comrades who had already begun to be forgotten, sorrowful children who would stare at your hands — they would come in, they would quickly place the guillotine in the middle of the room and suddenly, swoosh! my head would fall in the basket.

That was my sleep.

SELF-PORTRAIT

Each moment bewildered and inept, as though I had just arrived each moment—
from some other life ...

REPORT

O THE COUNTLESS ROADS I travelled, interminable undertakings! (days of my youth, where are you?) — the wind trembles from the everlasting farewells — each moment you come to blows with so many events — each year a new life awaits you with no time to get to know it — complicated matters, intrigues, mysteries, actions which remained in the dark for years and were brought to light when it was too late for anything, handshakes premeditated like crimes, weathervanes like the hands of the drowned and the terror which strikes you like a spanner in the face — oblivion always wins out.

And suddenly, as the sun sets on the horizon, you stand devoutly at the corner of the road, while the far-off bells atone for the day.

VARIATION IN AN OLDER TESTAMENT

As for the Testament which made me an inheritor
of the earth, out of fear that they might steal it from me, I
ripped it to a thousand pieces and scattered it to the winds.
But I retained the most beautiful words
which I use when speaking with you.

At that time Martha, who was sitting next to me, spread out an old blanket, possibly to cover the trivialities or the subterfuges — for in the depths of your degradation you always find an unexpected tranquillity, an appeasing discharge of some old debt, but a debt to whom? and incurred when? — and only when you have lost everything can you have a ready answer for everything — and as horrid things were taking place all around me, I stood calm, defending at great risk the mystery of my life —

just like poetry which is another form of dying.

THE GREAT SIN

ONE WAY or another I would have done great things in my life, but I was born very preoccupied — I mean to say (to say what? and who would understand?) — I was living at that time in a squalid hotel near the station, the trains would depart quickly like the Ages — at night a gunshot from the past would suddenly be heard and the nostalgia would kill me — meanwhile the withered maid was laying the sheets, enveloped in the dense mystery of a life squandered without reason — and I would remember my mother saying to me, 'My son, there is only one great sin,' and I understood, because there exist very few words in the world — just as the most beautiful stories will be told about us

when there will no longer be anyone to hear them.

FAVOURS

GOD TOOK PITY on those who were greatly humiliated and gave them a previous life too —
hence now they remember more.

WINTERTIME MISUNDERSTANDINGS

To BE SURE, at bottom it was ridiculous — there I was, wearing two jackets and giving everyone the impression that I was cold — 'You are wrong, you criminals!' I told them. 'How else could I bury naked
    the Other you killed within me?'

TEXTS OF OUR FORTHCOMING LIFE

As FOR the details of this colossal mistake which is my life, they will finally remain unknown (and even more so to myself) — and only memories supported me while on the road, like musical instruments which are blind but lead us by the hand — or I'd fall in love with a star (so that I may have one more reason to die) — let's leaf through, then, these humble lamps of the earth, given that the heavens are difficult to decipher — I know you and you know me — our acquaintance goes back to an old written-off crime — who remembers it? when did it happen? who killed whom? — everything blurred, inexplicable

and someday a beautiful text will be written without a trace of truth, and perhaps this will give us the solution to the enigma.

NOCTURNAL SENSIBILITIES

Quiet rain, the lit up windows of the coffee-houses
a harmonica somewhere in the distance pushes the night
   deeper into infinity
and the poets sleep like thieves, with ears strained towards
   the unknown word.

ALARM SIGNAL

SUDDENLY I SAW Jacob entering the room through the mirror — I was shaken — 'How is it possible?' I said to him — 'Don't you see,' he replied, 'all is lost' — in this way I tried to save my soul or at least get a little sleep, because not even for a day did I open my eyes without the mystery growing greater still — meanwhile night would fall and the gardens would fill with mothers and the cisterns with early fallen leaves so that I may hide better — and late at night I would lock the door and hear the sick children turning over in their sleep.

Had they thrown a boat into my brain it would have run aground.

THE CRIME

NATURALLY I don't remember the details, but I must concede that it was in every sense of the word a 'family' crime. We are in the large living room of some other person's house together with my mother, sister and three brothers. The bus which brought us was dilapidated and by the time we arrived we were already exasperated. We then passed the evening with sweet waltzes and even worse thoughts. But why did we commit that horrific crime? Out of revenge? Out of a mania for destruction? Or perhaps because they had cast doubt on my belief in life after death (something which always made my blood boil)? And who out of the whole family gave the final and decisive blow? I looked at them one by one. Mother always stood at the back, pale. Tears began to well up in me. 'May I have this dance, mother?' I said to her — for here, by way of parenthesis, I must remind you, Satan, that I was not born already advanced in age...

CRITIQUE

THERE ARE TIMES when a great adventure traverses the road — I run to catch up with it, I trip up, others trample on me, I get up again, but I am overtaken by malice — 'No,' I say, 'I'm better off going to Kyrilos's' — we drink tea in the kitchen and remain silent till the morning — what else is one to do in this world? And the proof: so many gold-bound volumes of tedious History.

HEAVENLY ACQUAINTANCES

That same evening I made the acquaintance of the unforgettable Matthias (you remember him): a former terrorist, a gentle soul and non-existent person — besides, the resemblance was so remarkable that you would walk quietly into the room in case everything suddenly disappeared — 'I am an anarchist,' he would say, but in reality he was so defenceless that he would provoke awe just like the icons — exiled forever to the heavens, he would descend from there especially at the end of the day, solely for the lovely evening friendships with the children on the street corners, a little before mother would call them in for supper.

A QUESTION OF LOCATION

IN THE EVENINGS friends go looking for me in the coffee-houses, where they find a glass of cognac emptying slowly slowly on its own —
but what else was I to do given that I existed always
on the other side of life.

LETHAL GAME

I COULDN'T REMEMBER how I got here, in this room with the blinding light — I was sitting at a table, and opposite me was my fellow card player, a man unknown to me — we'd been playing for hours, perhaps even years — the pack of cards: worn out, ominous — not a cent of my money was left — 'I raise you my past!' I shouted — the other's eyelids were lowered murderously — he dealt the cards — I lost — 'I raise you all my future days!' I howled —

and then I noticed that I was all alone on a deserted building lot, and in the distance the city lay destroyed — from what? and I, who was I? where was I going? — 'Sweet mother of Christ,' I whispered, 'at last all is finished.

Now I can start over again.'

INDEX

OF

TITLES